Handy Crafts

PERFECT PARTIES

Gillian Souter

Gareth Stevens Publishing
A WORLD ALMANAC EDUCATION GROUP COMPANY

✶ Before You Start ✶

Some of these projects can get messy, so make sure your work area is covered with newspaper. For projects that need paint, you can use acrylic paint, poster paint, or any other kind of paint that is labeled nontoxic. Ask an adult to help you find paints that are safe to use. You will also need an adult's help to make some of the projects, especially for cutting with a craft knife or using the oven for baking.

Please visit our web site at: www.garethstevens.com
For a free color catalog describing Gareth Stevens' list of high-quality books and multimedia programs, call 1-800-542-2595 (USA) or 1-800-461-9120 (Canada).
Gareth Stevens Publishing's Fax: (414) 332-3567.

Library of Congress Cataloging-in-Publication Data

Souter, Gillian
    Perfect parties / by Gillian Souter
       p. cm. -- (Handy crafts)
    Includes bibliographical references and index.
    ISBN 0-8368-2822-4 (lib. bdg.)
    1. Handicraft. 2. Entertaining. [1. Parties. 2. Party decorations.
    3. Entertaining. 4. Handicraft.] I. Title. II. Series.
    TT157 .S645 2001
    793.2'1--dc21   00-052244

This edition first published in 2001 by
Gareth Stevens Publishing
A World Almanac Education Group Company
330 West Olive Street, Suite 100
Milwaukee, Wisconsin 53212 USA

This U.S. edition © 2001 by Gareth Stevens, Inc. Original edition published as *Party Time* in 1999 by Off the Shelf Publishing, 32 Thomas Street, Lewisham NSW 2049, Australia. Projects, text, and layout © 1999 by Off the Shelf Publishing. Additional end matter © 2001 by Gareth Stevens, Inc.

Illustrations: Clare Watson
Photographs: Andre Martin
Cover design: Joel Bucaro
Gareth Stevens editor: Monica Rausch

Printed in the United States of America

1 2 3 4 5 6 7 8 9 05 04 03 02 01

Contents

Get Set

One of the best parts of throwing a party is planning it! Here are some ideas.

Choose a theme for your party. Look on pages 46 and 47 for ideas, or think of your own theme. Use your imagination to make your party unique.

Send out invitations to your friends to let them know where and when you will have your party. Also, tell them if you want them to wear something special.

Decorate your party room with streamers and paper chains. You also can tie balloons onto fences or tree branches outside.

What games will you play or what fun things will you make at the party? Plan activities ahead of time, so your party will run smoothly.

You can give prizes to guests who win games — or to all of your guests. This book has lots of ideas for prizes.

Do not forget food! Make sure you have something for your guests to eat. You can also give your guests treats to take home.

5

Let's Party!

Stencils can help you make lots of invitations — all with the same design.

You Will Need

- scissors
- colored cardboard
- craft knife
- ruler
- thin cardboard
- pencil
- thick paints
- saucers
- sponge
- markers and stickers

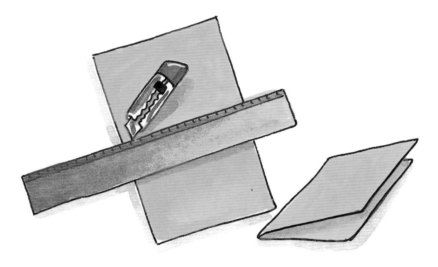

1 Cut rectangles out of colored cardboard. Ask an adult to run a craft knife lightly across the middle of each rectangle. Fold the rectangle along the cut.

2 Now you have invitations. Cut a piece of thin cardboard slightly smaller than the front of the invitations. Draw a party design on this piece of cardboard.

3 Ask an adult to cut out the design with a craft knife to make a stencil. Place the stencil over the front of the invitation.

4 Pour each color of paint onto a saucer. Dip one corner of a sponge into paint, then dab the paint onto the design. Use a different corner of the sponge to dab on each color.

5 When the paint is dry, use markers to add extra details to the design. You can also add stickers.

★ **Helpful Hint** ★
Be sure to write information about the party, such as the party's date and time, inside the card.

7

Paper Capers

Colorful crepe paper chains can make your party room festive and fun.

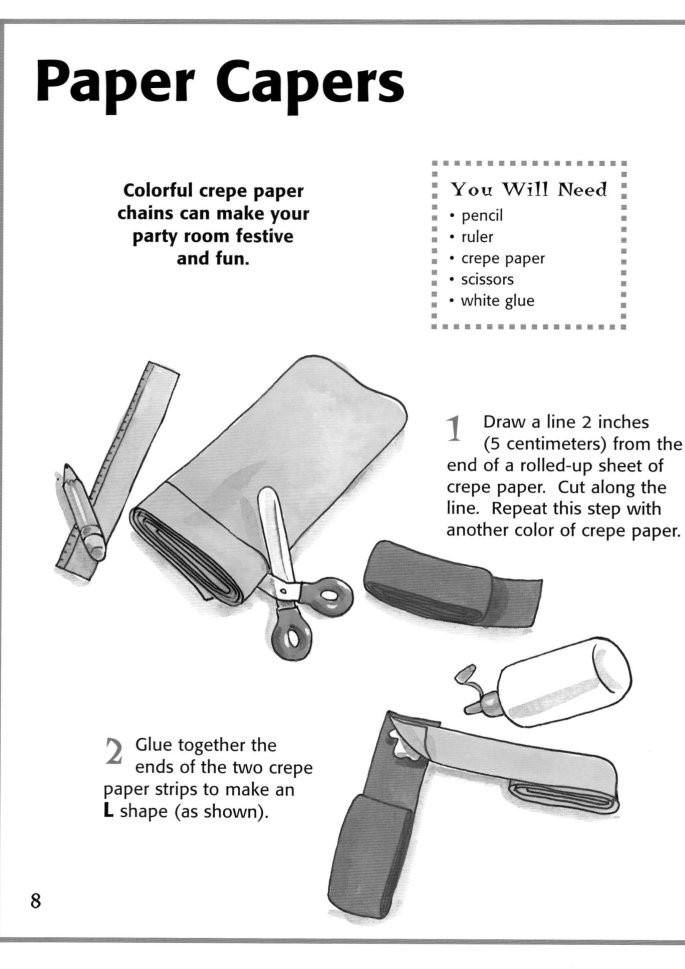

1 Draw a line 2 inches (5 centimeters) from the end of a rolled-up sheet of crepe paper. Cut along the line. Repeat this step with another color of crepe paper.

2 Glue together the ends of the two crepe paper strips to make an **L** shape (as shown).

3   Fold the vertical strip over the glued ends. Then fold the horizontal strip across. Keep folding the strips over and across each other.

4   When you reach the end of a strip, glue the two strips together. Trim off any extra crepe paper. Let the glue dry before you pull open the chain.

★ **Bright Idea** ★
Glue together lots of crepe paper chains to make longer chains.

9

Jelly Fellas

Hang a few of these crazy jellyfish creatures around the room to liven up your party.

1 Cut four or five long pieces of paper streamers. Punch a hole in one end of each piece.

2 Ask an adult to poke two holes in the bottom of a plastic cup with the point of a compass.

3 Pull a piece of string through the holes in the streamers.

10

4 Pull each end of the string
through a hole in the cup
and tie the ends in a knot.

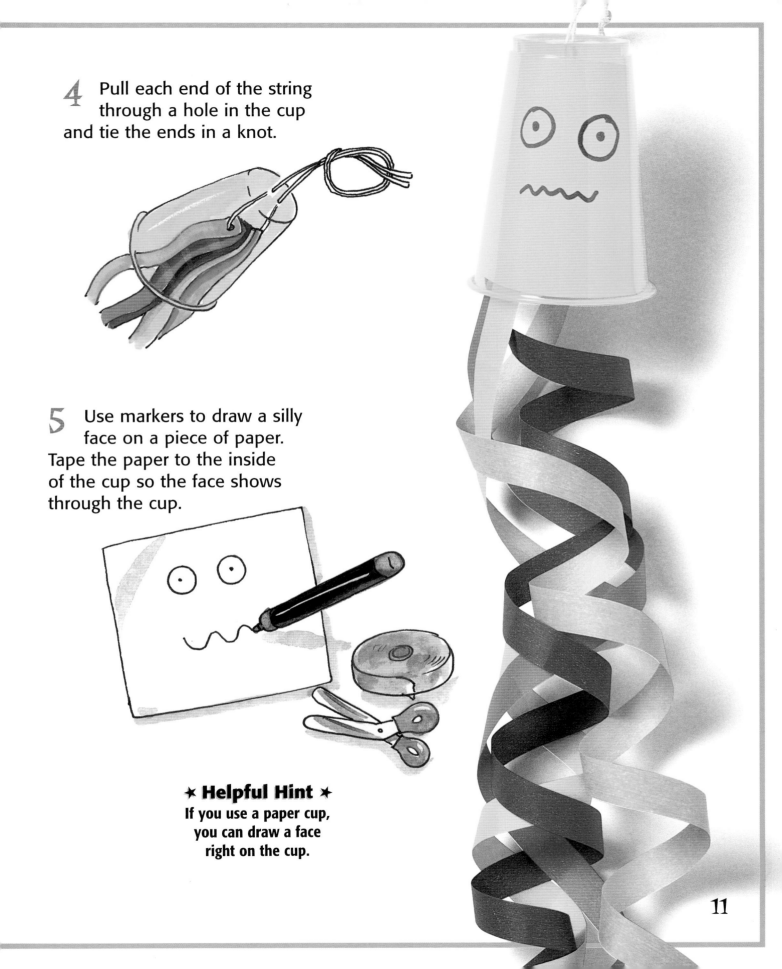

5 Use markers to draw a silly
face on a piece of paper.
Tape the paper to the inside
of the cup so the face shows
through the cup.

★ **Helpful Hint** ★
If you use a paper cup,
you can draw a face
right on the cup.

11

Hair Wear

Instead of passing out party hats, let your guests create their own clever headbands.

1 Wrap a piece of string around your head and cut the string to the size of your head. Cut narrow strips of colored cardboard slightly longer than the string. You will need two strips of cardboard for each headband.

2 Cut feather shapes out of cardboard. Snip along the sides of each shape to make fringes.

3 Scrunch pieces of aluminum foil around the ends of pipe cleaners to make antennae.

12

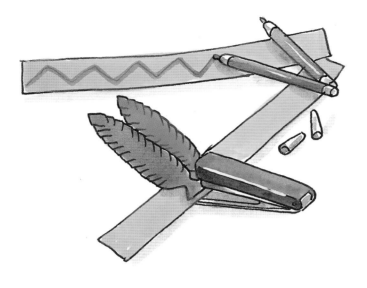

4 When your party guests arrive, ask each guest to decorate a cardboard strip with markers. Staple two feathers or antennae onto another cardboard strip.

5 Lay the two strips together with the feathers or antennae between them. Ask an adult to staple together the ends of a headband to fit each guest's head.

13

Mystery Masks

These goofy disguises will keep your guests giggling.

You Will Need
- pencil
- two sheets of tracing paper
- clear tape
- glue stick
- thin black cardboard
- scissors
- cardboard egg carton
- paints and paintbrush

1 Trace the shape below on one sheet of tracing paper. On the other sheet, trace the shape again. Tape the two sheets of tracing paper together so the tracings form a pair of eyeglasses.

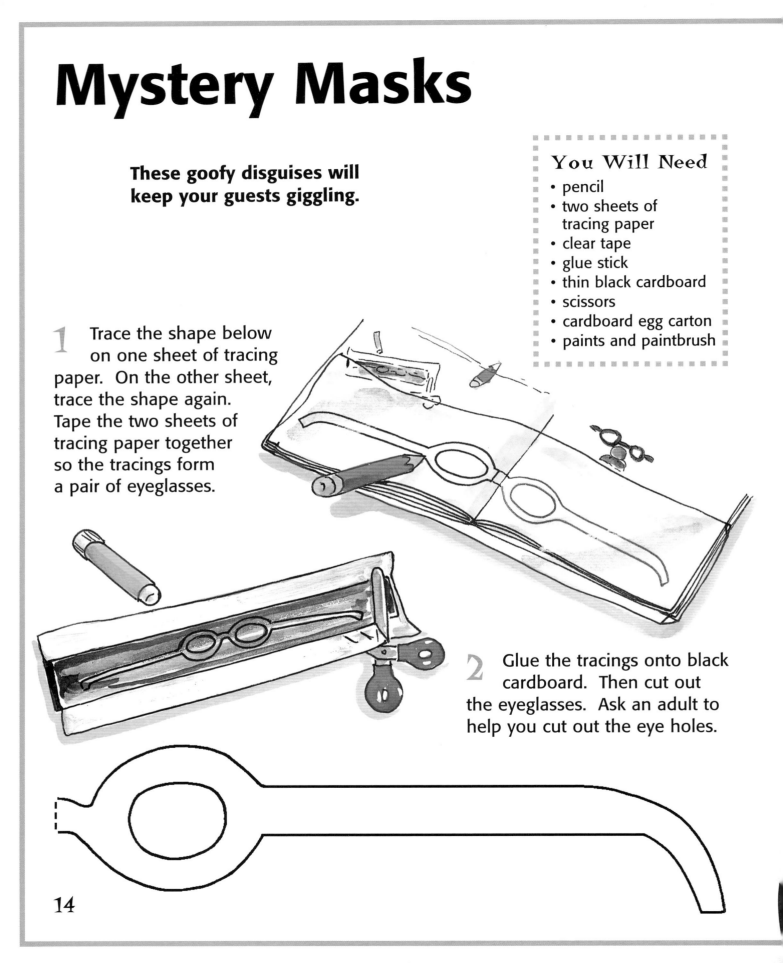

2 Glue the tracings onto black cardboard. Then cut out the eyeglasses. Ask an adult to help you cut out the eye holes.

14

3   To make a nose, cut one cup off of a cardboard egg carton. Paint the outside of the cup.

4   Cut a mustache shape out of black cardboard. Make cuts along the bottom of the shape (as shown). Tape the top of the mustache inside the bottom of the nose.

5   Tape the top of the nose to the back of the eyeglasses. Then fold back the arms of the eyeglasses and put on your funny disguise.

★ **Helpful Hint** ★
Change the length
of the arms to
fit your head.

15

It's a Wrap!

**This gift is really a game!
Your guests will be
unwrapping again
and again.**

You Will Need
- cloth tape measure
- scissors
- tissue paper
- glue stick
- colored paper
- pen or pencil
- small prize
- wrapping paper
- ribbon

1   Use a tape measure to measure
    around your head. For each guest,
cut a wide strip of tissue paper a little
longer than this measurement.

2   Overlap the ends of each
    tissue paper strip and glue
them together to make a hat.
Cut triangles or other shapes
along the top edge of each hat.

3 Cut a small square of colored paper for each guest. On each square, write a silly command, such as "quack like a duck" or "sing a funny song."

4 Wrap a small prize, such as candy, stickers, or a toy, in wrapping paper.

5 Wrap the prize, along with a hat and a note, in another layer of paper. Keep wrapping, putting a hat and a note in each layer.

★ How to Play ★

Guests pass the present to music. Whoever has it when the music stops unwraps a layer and obeys a command.

Sweet Creatures

This colorful dough is very sweet — but don't let your guests eat it!

1 Use a fork to lightly beat the white of one egg. Sift in powdered sugar and stir the mixture into a dough.

2 Knead the dough until it is smooth. Then divide the dough into three balls. Put each ball in a separate bowl.

3 Add two drops of food coloring to each bowl and knead the coloring into the dough. Wrap each ball of dough with plastic wrap. Keep the dough in the refrigerator until party time.

4 You and your guests can shape the dough into creatures with your fingers or with cookie cutters.

5 Decorate your sweet creatures with small pieces of dough or designs made with a fork.

★ **Bright Idea** ★
Use small pieces of candy and licorice strips to add features to your creatures.

19

A Sure Hit

A piñata is always a party favorite. Treat your guests to a shower of candy.

You Will Need
- balloon
- vegetable oil
- white glue and water
- newspaper
- paintbrush
- pin and scissors
- acrylic paints
- ribbon
- candy

1 Blow up a balloon and tie a knot at the end. Rub vegetable oil all over the balloon.

2 Mix together equal amounts of white glue and water. Tear some newspaper into thin strips. Lay each strip on the balloon, then brush over it with the glue mixture. Overlap the strips as you go.

3 Cover the entire balloon, except the knot, with three layers of newspaper strips. Brush more glue mixture over each layer.

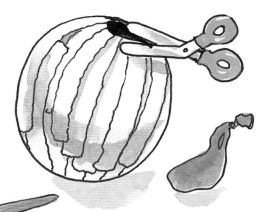

4 Leave the balloon in a dry place for two days. When the newspaper strips are dry, pop the balloon with a pin and pull it out. Neatly trim around the opening where the balloon's knot used to be.

5 Now you have a piñata. Paint the piñata white. When this paint is dry, paint on bright colors. After all the paint has dried, fill the piñata with lots of candy.

6 Ask an adult to poke two holes, across from each other, near the piñata's opening. Pull a ribbon through the holes and tie the ends together.

★ How to Play ★
Hang the piñata outdoors and let your guests take turns hitting it with a stick or a baseball bat. When it breaks, candy will fly everywhere!

21

Flutterball

Here's a soft ball you might be allowed to throw indoors. Its long tail flutters through the air.

1 Cut a square of fabric 10 inches by 10 inches (25 cm by 25 cm) — or just use a large handkerchief.

2 Roll an old sock into a ball and lay the sock in the center of the fabric square.

22

3 Bring the edges of the fabric up around the sock and hold them together with a rubber band.

4 Cut a long piece of ribbon. Tie the ribbon around the fabric, over the rubber band, and let the ends hang down. Tie on more pieces of ribbon so the ball will flutter when you throw it.

★ **Bright Idea** ★
If you don't have ribbons, use long strips of colorful fabric.

23

Make and Shake

Your party will shake, rattle, and roll to the music of these tambourines!

1 Before the party, tear tissue paper into small squares and cut long pieces of curling ribbon.

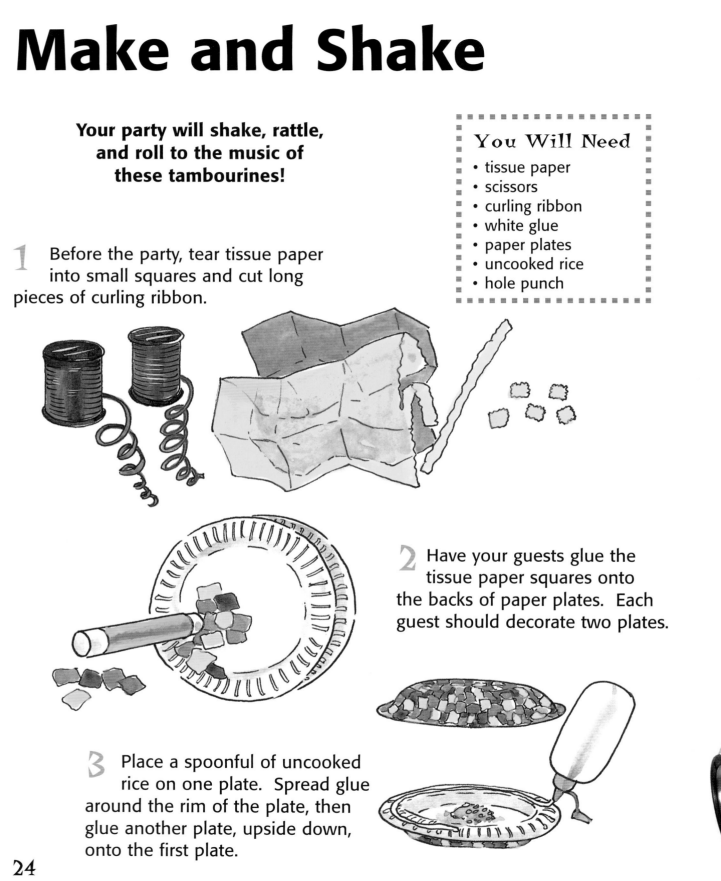

2 Have your guests glue the tissue paper squares onto the backs of paper plates. Each guest should decorate two plates.

3 Place a spoonful of uncooked rice on one plate. Spread glue around the rim of the plate, then glue another plate, upside down, onto the first plate.

24

4 Let the glue dry, then punch a hole near the edge of the plates.

5 Pull pieces of curling ribbon halfway through the hole and knot the ribbons near the edge of the plates.

★ **Bright Idea** ★
Use dry beans instead of rice to shake a different tune.

Gone Fishing

Let your guests try their luck at this fishing game. With a magnet for a hook, they can attract a lot of fish.

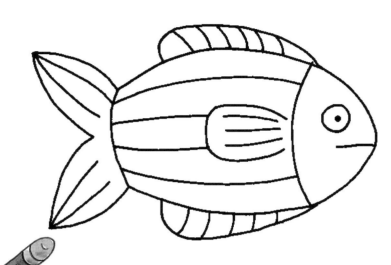

1 Place tracing paper over the fish pattern above. Use a soft pencil to trace the fish. Turn the tracing paper over onto a piece of colored cardboard. Draw over the pencil lines to transfer the fish pattern onto the cardboard.

2 Darken the pencil lines on the cardboard with a black marker. Repeat steps 1 and 2 to make lots of fish.

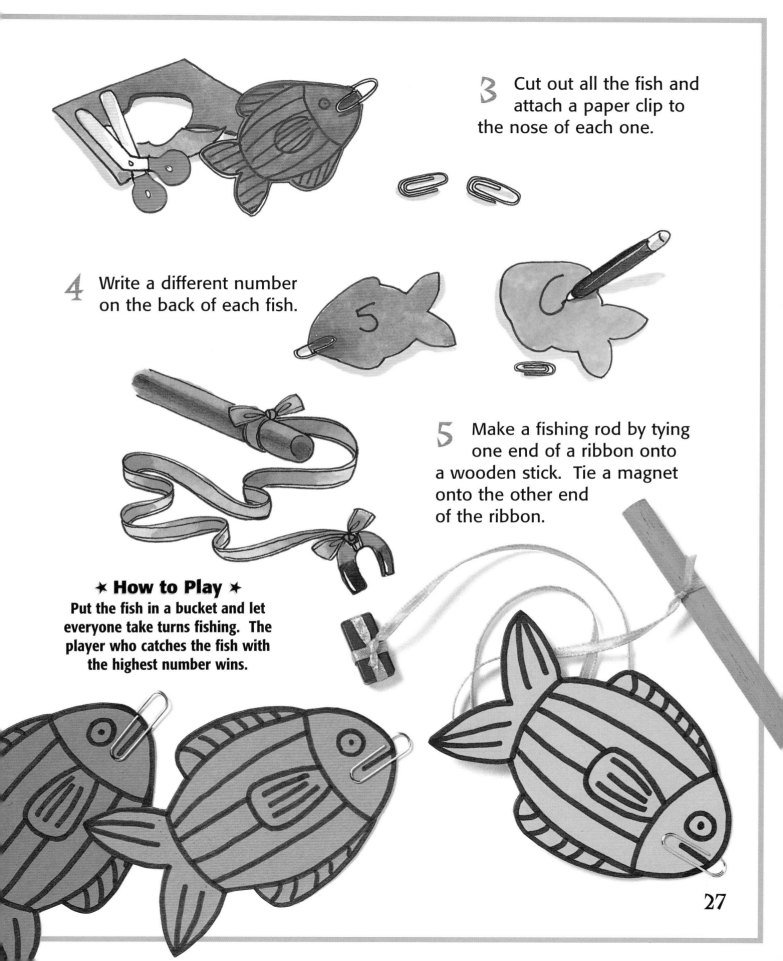

3 Cut out all the fish and attach a paper clip to the nose of each one.

4 Write a different number on the back of each fish.

5

5 Make a fishing rod by tying one end of a ribbon onto a wooden stick. Tie a magnet onto the other end of the ribbon.

★ **How to Play** ★
Put the fish in a bucket and let everyone take turns fishing. The player who catches the fish with the highest number wins.

Super Star

Give the star of the party this special badge — or make star badges for all your guests!

You Will Need
- tracing paper
- pencil
- scissors
- straight pins
- colored felt
- small lid and a glass
- pinking shears
- needle and thread
- large safety pin

1 Place tracing paper over the star pattern on this page. Use a pencil to trace the star. Then cut out the star.

2 Pin the paper star onto a piece of felt. Cut out a felt star by snipping inward along each point, toward the center of the star.

28

3 Use a small lid to trace a circle onto felt. Cut out the circle. On a different color of felt, draw a larger circle around a glass. Use pinking shears to cut out the larger circle.

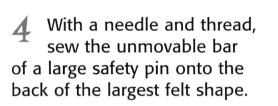

4 With a needle and thread, sew the unmovable bar of a large safety pin onto the back of the largest felt shape.

5 Stack the felt shapes in order of size, with the largest shape on the bottom. Sew some stitches through the center of the stack to hold the felt shapes together.

★ **Helpful Hint** ★
You might have to ask an adult for help with the sewing.

Key Critters

Crazy key ring creatures make perfect prizes for party games — or great gifts for your guests.

1 Mix flour and salt in a bowl. Slowly stir in water. Mix until a soft dough forms. Knead the dough until it is smooth.

★ Bright Idea ★
Use cardboard shapes instead of cookie cutters. Lay the shapes on the dough, then cut around them with a dull knife.

2 Ask an adult to set the oven at 350° Fahrenheit (180° Celsius). Use a rolling pin to roll out the dough until it is about as thick as a cookie. Press cookie cutters into the dough to make fun shapes.

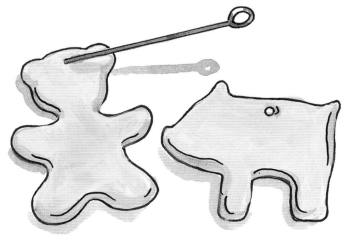

3 Gently place the shapes on a cookie sheet. Use a skewer to make a hole at the top of each shape. Ask an adult to bake the shapes in the oven for 2 hours.

4 Let the shapes cool, then paint them bright colors. Let the paint dry.

5 Thread a narrow ribbon through the hole in one of the shapes, then through a key ring. Tie the ends of the ribbon in a knot. Repeat this step with each shape.

31

Places, Please!

Let these eight-legged octopuses show your guests exactly where to sit.

You Will Need
- scissors
- pipe cleaners
- ruler
- black pen or marker
- white paper
- white glue
- thin cardboard

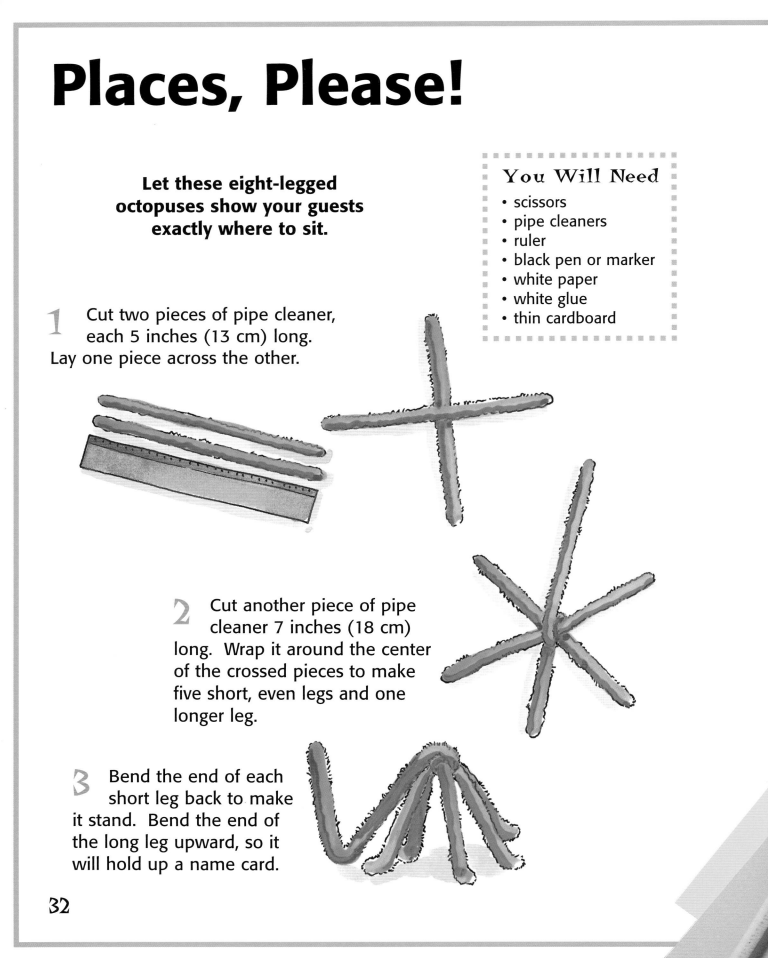

1 Cut two pieces of pipe cleaner, each 5 inches (13 cm) long. Lay one piece across the other.

2 Cut another piece of pipe cleaner 7 inches (18 cm) long. Wrap it around the center of the crossed pieces to make five short, even legs and one longer leg.

3 Bend the end of each short leg back to make it stand. Bend the end of the long leg upward, so it will hold up a name card.

32

4 Cut another 7-inch (18-cm) piece of pipe cleaner. Wrap the middle of it around the place where all the pipe cleaners meet to form a head. Bend the ends down to make two extra legs.

5 To make eyes, draw small circles on white paper and cut them out. Make a black dot in the center of each circle. Glue two eyes onto the head of each octopus.

6 Cut a cardboard square for each guest. Write one guest's name on each square. Let each octopus hold a name.

★ Helpful Hint ★
Arrange the name card holders on the table before your party.

33

Snappy Napkins

Pretty printed party napkins will prepare your guests for a fancy feast.

1 Use a black marker to draw a shape on a sponge. Cut out the shape.

2 Glue the sponge shape onto a square of thick cardboard to make a stamp.

3 Unfold a paper napkin and lay it flat on some newspaper. Pour paint onto a paper plate.

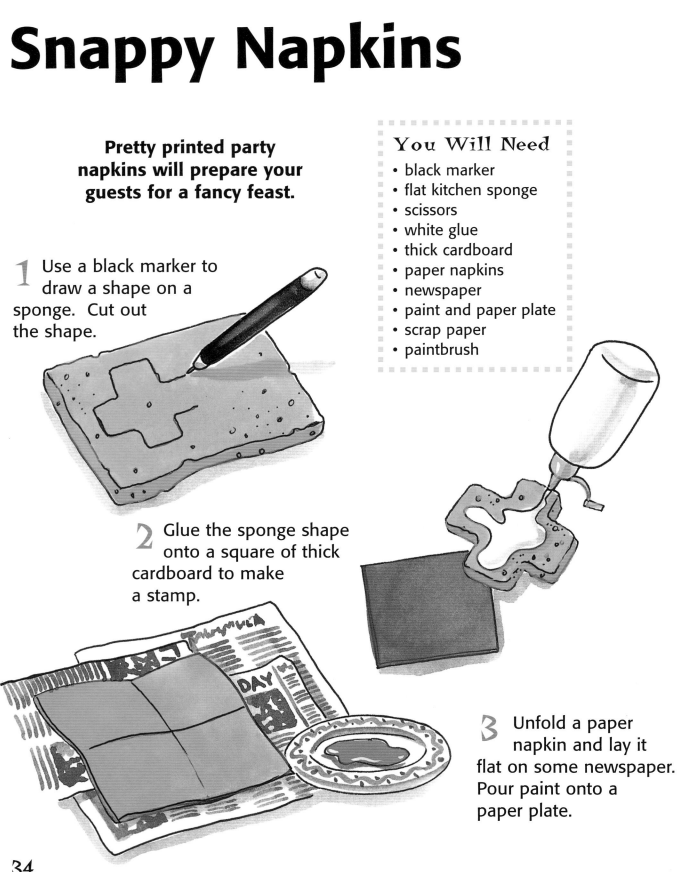

34

4   Holding onto the cardboard square, press the sponge into the paint. Test your stamp on a piece of scrap paper. You may need to brush paint onto the sponge to cover it evenly.

5   After you have tested the stamp, print the design on the paper napkin. You might be able to make several prints before the sponge needs more paint.

★ **Bright Idea** ★
Design napkins that go with your party's theme.

Jell-O Jewels

**Your guests will
gobble up these jiggly
Jell-O treats!**

You Will Need
- knife
- oranges
- spoon
- muffin pan
- two bowls
- Jell-O powder

1 Ask an adult to cut
several oranges in
half, from their stems
to their bottoms.

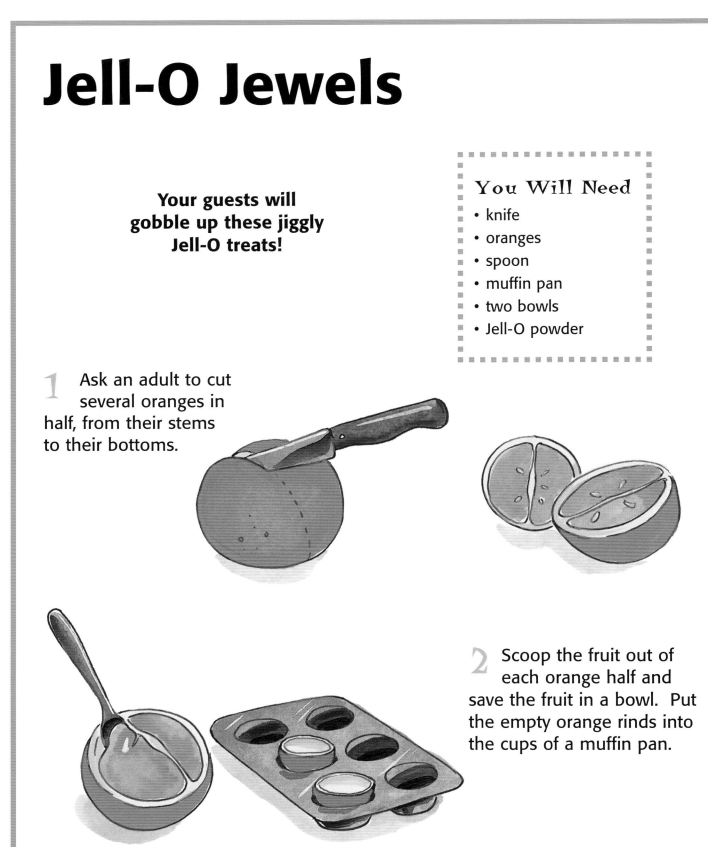

2 Scoop the fruit out of
each orange half and
save the fruit in a bowl. Put
the empty orange rinds into
the cups of a muffin pan.

36

3 Pour Jell-O powder into a bowl. Add hot water. (See the Jell-O package for measurements.) Stir the mixture until the powder has dissolved in the water.

4 Let the Jell-O cool slightly, then pour it into the orange rinds. Put the pan full of rinds into the refrigerator.

5 When the Jell-O has set, cut each orange rind in half to make quarters. Arrange the quarters on a colorful plate.

★ Bright Idea ★
Use the fruit from the oranges to make orange juice.

Claim Your Cookie

You Will Need
- sieve
- 1 ½ cups (250 g) powdered sugar
- bowl
- warm water
- spoon
- sugar cookies
- food coloring
- pastry bag
- small candy pieces

Nobody will miss out on dessert when you give each guest a special cookie.

1 Sift powdered sugar into a bowl. Add 1 tablespoon of warm water. Stir the mixture until it is smooth. Add more water if you need it. You now have a tasty frosting.

2 Spread some frosting onto a cookie with the bottom of a spoon. Let the frosting harden. Frost a cookie for each party guest.

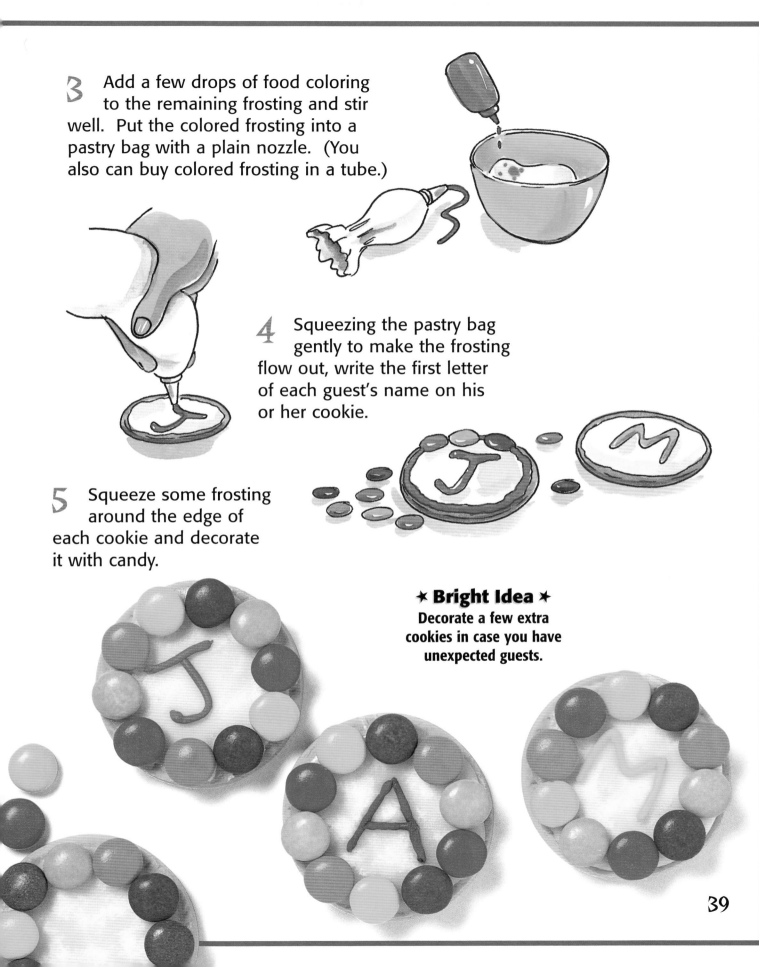

3 Add a few drops of food coloring to the remaining frosting and stir well. Put the colored frosting into a pastry bag with a plain nozzle. (You also can buy colored frosting in a tube.)

4 Squeezing the pastry bag gently to make the frosting flow out, write the first letter of each guest's name on his or her cookie.

5 Squeeze some frosting around the edge of each cookie and decorate it with candy.

★ **Bright Idea** ★
Decorate a few extra cookies in case you have unexpected guests.

Pizza Pals

These personal pizzas will make party guests smile — and fill their tummies, too!

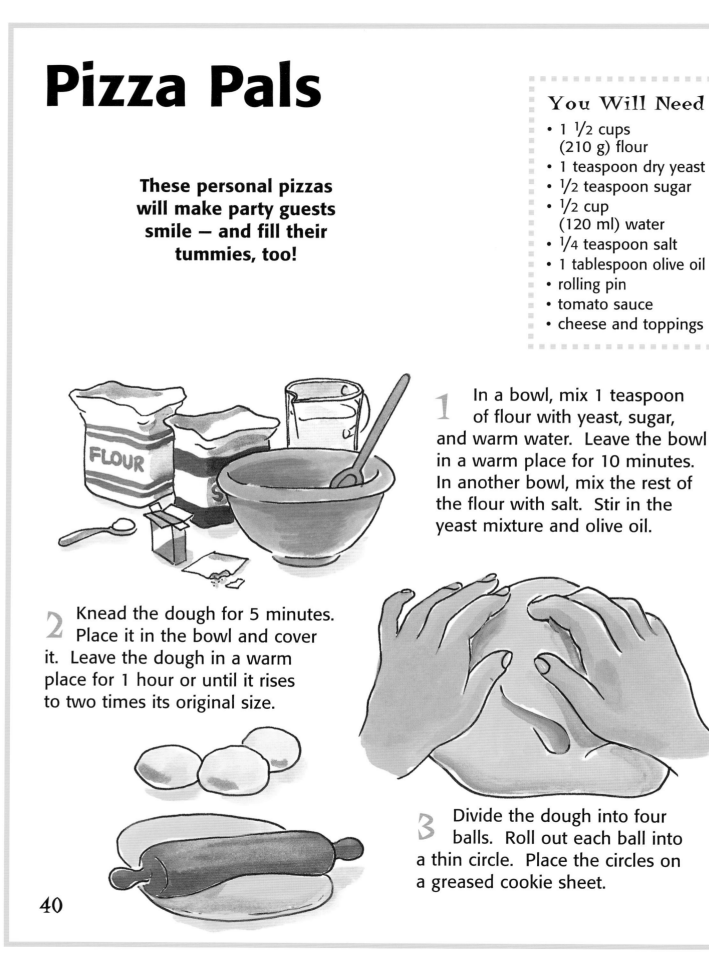

You Will Need
- 1 ½ cups (210 g) flour
- 1 teaspoon dry yeast
- ½ teaspoon sugar
- ½ cup (120 ml) water
- ¼ teaspoon salt
- 1 tablespoon olive oil
- rolling pin
- tomato sauce
- cheese and toppings

1 In a bowl, mix 1 teaspoon of flour with yeast, sugar, and warm water. Leave the bowl in a warm place for 10 minutes. In another bowl, mix the rest of the flour with salt. Stir in the yeast mixture and olive oil.

2 Knead the dough for 5 minutes. Place it in the bowl and cover it. Leave the dough in a warm place for 1 hour or until it rises to two times its original size.

3 Divide the dough into four balls. Roll out each ball into a thin circle. Place the circles on a greased cookie sheet.

40

4 Spread tomato sauce over the circles of dough. Sprinkle grated cheese over the sauce.

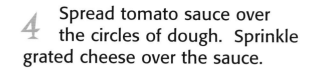

5 Make a face on each pizza with olives, pepperoni, tomatoes, green peppers, and other toppings.

6 Ask an adult to preheat the oven to 425° F (220° C). Bake the pizzas for 10 to 12 minutes.

★ Helpful Hint ★
This recipe makes four pizza pals. To make four more, you need twice as much dough!

Fake Cake

This cleverly crafted birthday cake won't fool your guests — but a hidden treat inside it will surprise them!

You Will Need
- round box
- paints and paintbrush
- scissors
- crepe paper
- glue
- thread
- metal skewer
- candleholders and birthday candles
- candy

1 Take off the lid of a round box. Paint the outside of the box white. Then paint it a light color that looks like frosting.

2 Cut a long strip of crepe paper. Wrap the strip around the box and glue down the overlapping ends.

3 Cut squares of crepe paper. Fold each square back and forth like a fan.

42

4   Tie thread around the middle of each folded square. Spread out the sides of the squares to make butterfly shapes. Glue the shapes onto the crepe paper strip around the box.

5   Ask an adult to punch holes in the top of the box with a metal skewer. Poke candleholders, with candles in them, into the holes.

★ **Bright Idea** ★
Find a bowl that will fit under the box. Fill the bowl with candy and hide it under the box.

Goodies to Go

Be sure to thank your guests. Give them colorful cones of candy they can take home.

1 Tie one end of a piece of string onto a pencil. Hold the other end down on a corner of piece of scrap paper. Keeping the string taut, move the pencil to draw an arc.

2 Cut along the arc. Place this paper shape on foil-coated cardboard and draw around it. Cut out the cardboard shape. Snip off the pointed end.

44

3 Cut cellophane into a square that is much larger than the cardboard shape. Tape the cellophane onto the dull side of the cardboard, along the cardboard's straight sides. Cut off the top corner of the cellophane.

4 Roll the cardboard into a cone with its straight sides overlapping. Tape the sides together.

5 Fill the cone with candy. Tie the top of the cellophane together with ribbon.

★ **Helpful Hint** ★
Stuff crumpled cellophane into the bottom of the cone so the candy will not fall out.

45

Think Themes!

A theme can make your party unique! Make invitations, decorations, games, and food to match.

Red Riot
Ask guests to dress in red, make red decorations, eat strawberries and cherries, and bob for apples — or choose any other color you like.

Out of This World
Use lots of aluminum foil to decorate your party room. Have everyone make alien antennae. Make a round piñata and paint it to look like planet Earth.

Pirates and Mermaids

Give your party a sea theme with lots of crepe paper seaweed and cardboard fish. Have a treasure hunt for gold coins and play the fishing game on pages 26 and 27.

A Monster Meet

Have your friends dress up as scary monsters! Feed them green Jell-O and weird pizza faces. Play pin the nose on the monster.

Teddy Bears' Picnic

Ask guests to bring their own teddy bears. Give out prizes for the bear with the biggest ears or the fuzziest fur. Serve peanut butter-and-honey sandwiches.

Glossary

antennae: long, thin, movable "feelers" on the heads of most insects.

arc: a curved line that forms part of a circle.

cellophane: clear, thin, plasticlike material made of cellulose, a substance found in plants.

dissolved: mixed completely with a liquid.

horizontal: level; straight across.

knead: to press and squeeze over and over with the hands.

pinking shears: scissors with zigzag blades that make zigzag cuts.

rind: the hard, tough outer layer on some fruits, such as lemons and oranges.

sieve: a strainer with holes through which only the fine particles can pass.

skewer: a pointed stick used to hold meat together while the meat is roasting.

stencil: a piece of stiff paper or cardboard with a design cut into it. When paint is spread over the stencil, the design is printed on the surface beneath it.

taut: stretched or pulled tightly.

theme: a main topic, subject, or idea around which an event is planned.

transfer: to copy from one surface to another.

vertical: straight up and down.

More Craft Books by Gareth Stevens

Crafty Masks. Crafty Kids (series). Thomasina Smith

Food Crafts. Worldwide Crafts (series). Chris Deshpande

How to Have Fun with Letters. Art Smart (series). Christine Smith

Monsters and Extraterrestrials. Draw, Model, and Paint (series). Isidro Sánchez

Index